This Journal belongs to:

_____

Date:

_____

Ecclesiastes
journal

Teresa Hodge

Ecclesiastes Journal: Finding Meaning In Life

Copyright © 2019 Teresa Hodge

ISBN 9781723883194

Cover design: Jen Kline

Color pages: afewwords/Bigstock.com, p. 21, 69

                Alfadanz/Bigstock.com, p. 45

All scripture taken from the Bible (KJV)

Find Teresa Hodge on the web—

Blog: **LadiesDrawingNigh.org**

Facebook: **Facebook.com/LadiesDrawingNigh/**

Instagram: **Instagram.com/LadiesDrawingNigh/**

Pinterest: **Pinterest.com/LadiesDrawingNigh/**

Contents

Acknowledgements

There are so many who have prayed and encouraged me in the work and ministry of Ladies Drawing Nigh. And I praise God for each of you! It takes many working and praying together to accomplish God's purposes.

I am especially thankful for my husband, Todd, and our two daughters, Taylor and Mallory, who have graciously given me the time necessary for this ministry and encouraged me along the way.

Without the Lord and His wisdom, help, faithfulness, and provision, the Ladies Drawing Nigh ministry…and this journal…would not exist. Therefore, I dedicate this publication to our Saviour Jesus Christ. For He alone is worthy of praise! May He be glorified!

O magnify the LORD with me,
and let us exalt his name together.
Psalm 34:3

Introduction

Welcome to the **Ecclesiastes Journal: Finding Meaning In Life**. I'm so excited to study this book with you! For the next 3 weeks we will look into the book of Ecclesiastes together. And join Solomon in his desperate journey to discover what, if anything, could give meaning to this life.

JOIN THE LDN FELLOWSHIP!

This journal is the companion to our study online at **LadiesDrawingNigh.org.** But can be used as a stand-alone study aid, as well. All resources for this study will remain available under Bible Studies on the website.

Join us each weekday on **Facebook.com/LadiesDrawingNigh** and on **Instagram.com/LadiesDrawingNigh**. You won't want to miss the special fellowship while sharing with each other what we H.E.A.R. from God in our quiet time.

How To Use This Journal

This journal is created to be a keepsake in which you record your thoughts and discoveries as you read and study through the book of Ecclesiastes.

At **Ladies Drawing Nigh**, we will take a leisurely pace through the 12 chapters of Ecclesiastes so that we may take in all that God has for us each day. We will be reading approximately 1 chapter per day.

WHAT YOU DO

1) Each day, **after prayer** for the Spirit's wisdom and guidance, **read** the day's passage, **marking your Bible** in a way that *helps you* slow down and take notice of what God is saying. *There is no right or wrong way to do this.*

   See page 14 for suggestions on what kinds of information to look for and mark as you read. You might also like to jot down notes, or include your journaling art, in the Notes pages included at the end of each week.

   For help with marking and/or highlighting the passage, refer to my **Bible Marking Guide** and **Bible Highlighting Guide** online at *LadiesDrawingNigh.org.* They are available to print in bookmark form to be used as a handy reference in your journal.

2) Once you have read and/or marked your Bible passage, choose a verse(s) from the reading that spoke to you, and record on that day's **H.E.A.R. form** what you learned and heard from God. (See next page.)

H.E.A.R. *Bible Study Method*

My sheep hear my voice, and I know them, and they follow me: John 10:27
What did you **hear** today from the voice of His word? Psalm 103:20

His Word

Record here the verse(s) that spoke to you today.

Examine It

What did you observe about today's verse(s)? Record here 2 or 3 facts
you discovered as you looked more closely at the verse(s).
These facts may answer some of the 5 "W's" & an "H" questions...See p. 14.
What does the verse actually say? Did you learn something about God?

Apply It

How can you apply to your life what you learned from today's verse(s)?
Is there a command to obey? Is there a sin to confess?
Is there a promise you can claim?
Record here your plan to live out this verse.

Respond in Prayer

Write here your response to God...your prayer in response to His speaking
to you from His Word today.
Father, thank You for...   Father, please help me...

3) After filling in your H.E.A.R. form, take time to meditate on the day's **memory verse**. You may also like to spend a little time coloring one of the three **color pages** provided as you meditate on the day's passage.

4) After your quiet time with God, we'd love for you to join the discussion on *Facebook.com/LadiesDrawingNigh* or on *Instagram.com/LadiesDrawingNigh.* We need each other to learn and grow and be encouraged!

REMEMBER— The whole point of spending time in the Word and prayer is to **draw nigh to God**, to listen for and **hear your Shepherd's voice.** So, don't get so bogged down in your study…or in marking your passage…that you miss listening for and hearing Him.

I look forward to talking with you about Ecclesiastes as we study together this book that points us to God in our search for meaning in this life!

Drawing nigh to Him,

Teresa

BIBLE STUDY QUESTIONS TO PONDER

Who? Who is speaking? To whom? Who is this about?

What? What is happening? What event or topic is discussed? What do you learn about the event, topic, or people?

Look for—Key words and phrases, Lists, Comparisons and contrasts

What is the theme? Notice repeated words.

When? When does/will the event take place?

Where? Where does/will the event take place?

Why? Why does/will the event happen? Why is the topic mentioned?

How? How does/will the event unfold? How is the topic to be handled or made possible?

Where possible, find the answers to these questions in order to help you determine what the passage actually says. **Record your discoveries in box 'E' of the H.E.A.R. form.**

NOTE: Every season of life is different. So, on days when time is short, you could fill in the "H" box with your special verse. Then for the "E" box, simply re-write your special verse in your own words…or, as if you were explaining it to a child. Or, you may simply list a few truths, or facts, you notice in that verse.

Ecclesiastes

Reading Schedule

Week 1

[ ] Ecclesiastes 1
[ ] Ecclesiastes 2:1-11
[ ] Ecclesiastes 2:12-26
[ ] Ecclesiastes 3
[ ] Ecclesiastes 4

Week 2

[ ] Ecclesiastes 5
[ ] Ecclesiastes 6
[ ] Ecclesiastes 7:1-14
[ ] Ecclesiastes 7:15-29
[ ] Ecclesiastes 8

Week 3

[ ] Ecclesiastes 9
[ ] Ecclesiastes 10
[ ] Ecclesiastes 11
[ ] Ecclesiastes 12
[ ] Favorite passage

Overview of Ecclesiastes

The Book of Ecclesiastes is classified as part of the wisdom literature of the Bible, along with Job, Psalms, Proverbs, and Song of Solomon. Written around 935 B.C. by Solomon, King of Israel, Ecclesiastes is rather autobiographical in nature. Written toward the end of his life, Solomon describes his desperate journey to find meaning and significance in the many and varied pursuits of life "under the sun."

During Solomon's lifetime, he explored most every form of worldly pleasure there is. He sought fulfillment in…intellectual pursuit (1:13-18), laughter and fun (2:1), alcohol (2:3), work (2:4), wealth and possessions (2:7-8), and women (7:26-28). Only to discover that everything is, at best, only a temporary diversion.

King Solomon, with all his wealth and resources and power, had it all. And had done it all. And yet, found only world-weariness, emptiness, and regret. His conclusion?

> *Vanity of vanities, saith the Preacher, vanity of vanities; all is vanity.*
> *Ecclesiastes 1:2*

Solomon finally came to understand that without God all of life was meaningless, pointless. But with God, life is full, satisfying, and meaningful.

Under the inspiration of the Holy Spirit, Solomon pens the words of Ecclesiastes to urge us to learn from his mistakes. And to point us to a better life of meaning and significance…a life lived in the fear of God and obedience to His commands. Solomon sums up his search with these words…

> *Let us hear the conclusion of the whole matter: Fear God, and keep his*
> *commandments: for this is the whole duty of man. Ecclesiastes 12:13*

Christ in the Book of Ecclesiastes

The Bible is God's gift to us to reveal His Son Jesus Christ and His plan to redeem fallen man back unto Himself. Each book of the Bible teaches us more of who Jesus is. The Book of Ecclesiastes reveals Christ as the Meaning of Life, the answer to all the disappointments and vanities Solomon describes.

Key Verses:

Then I looked on all the works that my hands had wrought, and on the labour that I had laboured to do: and, behold, all was vanity and vexation of spirit, and there was no profit under the sun. Ecclesiastes 2:11

Let us hear the conclusion of the whole matter: Fear God, and keep his commandments: for this is the whole duty of man. Ecclesiastes 12:13

Outline

Introduction — 1:1-11
Solomon's Experiences — 1:12-6:9
Solomon's Conclusions — 6:10-12:8
Solomon's Final Advice — 12:9-14

You have made us
for yourself and
our hearts are
restless
until they find their
rest in Thee.

St. Augustine

Week 1

He hath made every thing
beautiful in his time:

Ecclesiastes 3:11a

Monday - Chapter 1

All Is Vanity

Vanity of vanities, saith the Preacher,
vanity of vanities: all is vanity.

Ecclesiastes 1:2

Chapter 1

(1) The words of the Preacher, the son of David, king in Jerusalem.

(2) Vanity of vanities, saith the Preacher, vanity of vanities; all is vanity.

(3) What profit hath a man of all his labour which he taketh under the sun?

(4) One generation passeth away, and another generation cometh: but the earth abideth for ever.

(5) The sun also ariseth, and the sun goeth down, and hasteth to his place where he arose.

(6) The wind goeth toward the south, and turneth about unto the north; it whirleth about continually, and the wind returneth again according to his circuits.

(7) All the rivers run into the sea; yet the sea is not full; unto the place from whence the rivers come, thither they return again.

(8) All things are full of labour; man cannot utter it: the eye is not satisfied with seeing, nor the ear filled with hearing.

(9) The thing that hath been, it is that which shall be; and that which is done is that which shall be done: and there is no new thing under the sun.

(10) Is there any thing whereof it may be said, See, this is new? it hath been already of old time, which was before us.

(11) There is no remembrance of former things; neither shall there be any remembrance of things that are to come with those that shall come after.

(12) I the Preacher was king over Israel in Jerusalem.

(13) And I gave my heart to seek and search out by wisdom concerning all things that are done under heaven: this sore travail hath God given to the sons of man to be exercised therewith.

(14) I have seen all the works that are done under the sun; and, behold, all is vanity and vexation of spirit.

(15) That which is crooked cannot be made straight: and that which is wanting cannot be numbered.

(16) I communed with mine own heart, saying, Lo, I am come to great estate, and have gotten more wisdom than all they that have been before me in Jerusalem: yea, my heart had great experience of wisdom and knowledge.

(17) And I gave my heart to know wisdom, and to know madness and folly: I perceived that this also is vexation of spirit.

(18) For in much wisdom is much grief: and he that increaseth knowledge increaseth sorrow.

H.E.A.R. *Bible Study Method*

My sheep hear my voice, and I know them, and they follow me: John 10:27
What did you **hear** today from the voice of His word? Psalm 103:20

His Word

Examine It

Apply It

Respond in Prayer

The Vanity of Self-Indulgence

I said in mine heart, Go to now,
I will prove thee with mirth,
therefore enjoy pleasure:
and, behold, this also is vanity.

Ecclesiastes 2:1

Chapter 2:1-11

(1) I said in mine heart, Go to now, I will prove thee with mirth, therefore enjoy pleasure: and, behold, this also is vanity.

(2) I said of laughter, It is mad: and of mirth, What doeth it?

(3) I sought in mine heart to give myself unto wine, yet acquainting mine heart with wisdom; and to lay hold on folly, till I might see what was that good for the sons of men, which they should do under the heaven all the days of their life.

(4) I made me great works; I builded me houses; I planted me vineyards:

(5) I made me gardens and orchards, and I planted trees in them of all kind of fruits:

(6) I made me pools of water, to water therewith the wood that bringeth forth trees:

(7) I got me servants and maidens, and had servants born in my house; also I had great possessions of great and small cattle above all that were in Jerusalem before me:

(8) I gathered me also silver and gold, and the peculiar treasure of kings and of the provinces: I gat me men singers and women singers, and the delights of the sons of men, as musical instruments, and that of all sorts.

(9) So I was great, and increased more than all that were before me in Jerusalem: also my wisdom remained with me.

(10) And whatsoever mine eyes desired I kept not from them, I withheld not my heart from any joy; for my heart rejoiced in all my labour: and this was my portion of all my labour.

(11) Then I looked on all the works that my hands had wrought, and on the labour that I had laboured to do: and, behold, all was vanity and vexation of spirit, and there was no profit under the sun.

H.E.A.R. *Bible Study Method*

My sheep hear my voice, and I know them, and they follow me: John 10:27

What did you **hear** today from the voice of His word? Psalm 103:20

His Word

Examine It

Apply It

Respond in Prayer

The Vanity of Toil

There is nothing better for a man, than that he should eat and drink, and that he should make his soul enjoy good in his labour. This also I saw, that it was from the hand of God.

Ecclesiastes 2:24

Chapter 2:12-26

(12) And I turned myself to behold wisdom, and madness, and folly: for what can the man do that cometh after the king? even that which hath been already done.

(13) Then I saw that wisdom excelleth folly, as far as light excelleth darkness.

(14) The wise man's eyes are in his head; but the fool walketh in darkness: and I myself perceived also that one event happeneth to them all.

(15) Then said I in my heart, As it happeneth to the fool, so it happeneth even to me; and why was I then more wise? Then I said in my heart, that this also is vanity.

(16) For there is no remembrance of the wise more than of the fool for ever; seeing that which now is in the days to come shall all be forgotten. And how dieth the wise man? as the fool.

(17) Therefore I hated life; because the work that is wrought under the sun is grievous unto me: for all is vanity and vexation of spirit.

(18) Yea, I hated all my labour which I had taken under the sun: because I should leave it unto the man that shall be after me.

(19) And who knoweth whether he shall be a wise man or a fool? yet shall he have rule over all my labour wherein I have laboured, and wherein I have shewed myself wise under the sun. This is also vanity.

(20) Therefore I went about to cause my heart to despair of all the labour which I took under the sun.

(21) For there is a man whose labour is in wisdom, and in knowledge, and in equity; yet to a man that hath not laboured therein shall he leave it for his portion. This also is vanity and a great evil.

(22) For what hath man of all his labour, and of the vexation of his heart, wherein he hath laboured under the sun?

(23) For all his days are sorrows, and his travail grief; yea, his heart taketh not rest in the night. This is also vanity.

(24) There is nothing better for a man, than that he should eat and drink, and that he should make his soul enjoy good in his labour. This also I saw, that it was from the hand of God.

(25) For who can eat, or who else can hasten hereunto, more than I?

(26) For God giveth to a man that is good in his sight wisdom, and knowledge, and joy: but to the sinner he giveth travail, to gather and to heap up, that he may give to him that is good before God. This also is vanity and vexation of spirit.

H.E.A.R. Bible Study Method

My sheep hear my voice, and I know them, and they follow me: John 10:27
What did you **hear** today from the voice of His word? Psalm 103:20

His Word

Examine It

Apply It

Respond in Prayer

A Time for Everything

To every thing there is a season,
and a time to every purpose under the heaven:

Ecclesiastes 3:1

Chapter 3

(1) To every thing there is a season, and a time to every purpose under the heaven:

(2) A time to be born, and a time to die; a time to plant, and a time to pluck up that which is planted;

(3) A time to kill, and a time to heal; a time to break down, and a time to build up;

(4) A time to weep, and a time to laugh; a time to mourn, and a time to dance;

(5) A time to cast away stones, and a time to gather stones together; a time to embrace, and a time to refrain from embracing;

(6) A time to get, and a time to lose; a time to keep, and a time to cast away;

(7) A time to rend, and a time to sew; a time to keep silence, and a time to speak;

(8) A time to love, and a time to hate; a time of war, and a time of peace.

(9) What profit hath he that worketh in that wherein he laboureth?

(10) I have seen the travail, which God hath given to the sons of men to be exercised in it.

(11) He hath made every thing beautiful in his time: also he hath set the world in their heart, so that no man can find out the work that God maketh from the beginning to the end.

(12) I know that there is no good in them, but for a man to rejoice, and to do good in his life.

(13) And also that every man should eat and drink, and enjoy the good of all his labour, it is the gift of God.

(14) I know that, whatsoever God doeth, it shall be for ever: nothing can be put to it, nor any thing taken from it: and God doeth it, that men should fear before him.

(15) That which hath been is now; and that which is to be hath already been; and God requireth that which is past.

(16) And moreover I saw under the sun the place of judgment, that wickedness was there; and the place of righteousness, that iniquity was there.

(17) I said in mine heart, God shall judge the righteous and the wicked: for there is a time there for every purpose and for every work.

(18) I said in mine heart concerning the estate of the sons of men, that God might manifest them, and that they might see that they themselves are beasts.

(19) For that which befalleth the sons of men befalleth beasts; even one thing befalleth them: as the one dieth, so dieth the other; yea, they have all one breath; so that a man hath no preeminence above a beast: for all is vanity.

(20) All go unto one place; all are of the dust, and all turn to dust again.

(21) Who knoweth the spirit of man that goeth upward, and the spirit of the beast that goeth downward to the earth?

(22) Wherefore I perceive that there is nothing better, than that a man should rejoice in his own works; for that is his portion: for who shall bring him to see what shall be after him?

H.E.A.R. *Bible Study Method*

My sheep hear my voice, and I know them, and they follow me: John 10:27

What did you **hear** today from the voice of His word? Psalm 103:20

His Word

Examine It

Apply It

Respond in Prayer

Evil Under the Sun

Two are better than one; because they have a good reward for their labour.

Ecclesiastes 4:9

Chapter 4

(1) So I returned, and considered all the oppressions that are done under the sun: and behold the tears of such as were oppressed, and they had no comforter; and on the side of their oppressors there was power; but they had no comforter.

(2) Wherefore I praised the dead which are already dead more than the living which are yet alive.

(3) Yea, better is he than both they, which hath not yet been, who hath not seen the evil work that is done under the sun.

(4) Again, I considered all travail, and every right work, that for this a man is envied of his neighbour. This is also vanity and vexation of spirit.

(5) The fool foldeth his hands together, and eateth his own flesh.

(6) Better is an handful with quietness, than both the hands full with travail and vexation of spirit.

(7) Then I returned, and I saw vanity under the sun.

(8) There is one alone, and there is not a second; yea, he hath neither child nor brother: yet is there no end of all his labour; neither is his eye satisfied with riches; neither saith he, For whom do I labour, and bereave my soul of good? This is also vanity, yea, it is a sore travail.

(9) Two are better than one; because they have a good reward for their labour.

(10) For if they fall, the one will lift up his fellow: but woe to him that is alone when he falleth; for he hath not another to help him up.

(11) Again, if two lie together, then they have heat: but how can one be warm alone?

(12) And if one prevail against him, two shall withstand him; and a threefold cord is not quickly broken.

(13) Better is a poor and a wise child than an old and foolish king, who will no more be admonished.

(14) For out of prison he cometh to reign; whereas also he that is born in his kingdom becometh poor.

(15) I considered all the living which walk under the sun, with the second child that shall stand up in his stead.

(16) There is no end of all the people, even of all that have been before them: they also that come after shall not rejoice in him. Surely this also is vanity and vexation of spirit.

H.E.A.R. *Bible Study Method*

My sheep hear my voice, and I know them, and they follow me: John 10:27

What did you **hear** today from the voice of His word? Psalm 103:20

His Word

Examine It

Apply It

Respond in Prayer

Notes

Notes

Week 2

*Two are better than one; because
they have a good reward for their labour.*

Ecclesiastes 4:9

Fear God

When thou vowest a vow unto God,
defer not to pay it;
for he hath no pleasure in fools:
pay that which thou hast vowed.

Ecclesiastes 5:4

Chapter 5

(1) Keep thy foot when thou goest to the house of God, and be more ready to hear, than to give the sacrifice of fools: for they consider not that they do evil.

(2) Be not rash with thy mouth, and let not thine heart be hasty to utter any thing before God: for God is in heaven, and thou upon earth: therefore let thy words be few.

(3) For a dream cometh through the multitude of business; and a fool's voice is known by multitude of words.

(4) When thou vowest a vow unto God, defer not to pay it; for he hath no pleasure in fools: pay that which thou hast vowed.

(5) Better is it that thou shouldest not vow, than that thou shouldest vow and not pay.

(6) Suffer not thy mouth to cause thy flesh to sin; neither say thou before the angel, that it was an error: wherefore should God be angry at thy voice, and destroy the work of thine hands?

(7) For in the multitude of dreams and many words there are also divers vanities: but fear thou God.

(8) If thou seest the oppression of the poor, and violent perverting of judgment and justice in a province, marvel not at the matter: for he that is higher than the highest regardeth; and there be higher than they.

(9) Moreover the profit of the earth is for all: the king himself is served by the field.

(10) He that loveth silver shall not be satisfied with silver; nor he that loveth abundance with increase: this is also vanity.

(11) When goods increase, they are increased that eat them: and what good is there to the owners thereof, saving the beholding of them with their eyes?

(12) The sleep of a labouring man is sweet, whether he eat little or much: but the abundance of the rich will not suffer him to sleep.

(13) There is a sore evil which I have seen under the sun, namely, riches kept for the owners thereof to their hurt.

(14) But those riches perish by evil travail: and he begetteth a son, and there is nothing in his hand.

(15) As he came forth of his mother's womb, naked shall he return to go as he came, and shall take nothing of his labour, which he may carry away in his hand.

(16) And this also is a sore evil, that in all points as he came, so shall he go: and what profit hath he that hath laboured for the wind?

(17) All his days also he eateth in darkness, and he hath much sorrow and wrath with his sickness.

(18) Behold that which I have seen: it is good and comely for one to eat and to drink, and to enjoy the good of all his labour that he taketh under the sun all the days of his life, which God giveth him: for it is his portion.

(19) Every man also to whom God hath given riches and wealth, and hath given him power to eat thereof, and to take his portion, and to rejoice in his labour; this is the gift of God.

(20) For he shall not much remember the days of his life; because God answereth him in the joy of his heart.

H.E.A.R. *Bible Study Method*

My sheep hear my voice, and I know them, and they follow me: John 10:27
What did you **hear** today from the voice of His word? Psalm 103:20

His Word

Examine It

Apply It

Respond in Prayer

Tuesday - Chapter 6

The Vanity of Wealth and Honor

All the labour of man is for his mouth,
and yet the appetite is not filled.

Ecclesiastes 6:7

Chapter 6

(1) There is an evil which I have seen under the sun, and it is common among men:

(2) A man to whom God hath given riches, wealth, and honour, so that he wanteth nothing for his soul of all that he desireth, yet God giveth him not power to eat thereof, but a stranger eateth it: this is vanity, and it is an evil disease.

(3) If a man beget an hundred children, and live many years, so that the days of his years be many, and his soul be not filled with good, and also that he have no burial; I say, that an untimely birth is better than he.

(4) For he cometh in with vanity, and departeth in darkness, and his name shall be covered with darkness.

(5) Moreover he hath not seen the sun, nor known any thing: this hath more rest than the other.

(6) Yea, though he live a thousand years twice told, yet hath he seen no good: do not all go to one place?

(7) All the labour of man is for his mouth, and yet the appetite is not filled.

(8) For what hath the wise more than the fool? what hath the poor, that knoweth to walk before the living?

(9) Better is the sight of the eyes than the wandering of the desire: this is also vanity and vexation of spirit.

(10) That which hath been is named already, and it is known that it is man: neither may he contend with him that is mightier than he.

(11) Seeing there be many things that increase vanity, what is man the better?

(12) For who knoweth what is good for man in this life, all the days of his vain life which he spendeth as a shadow? for who can tell a man what shall be after him under the sun?

H.E.A.R. *Bible Study Method*

My sheep hear my voice, and I know them, and they follow me: John 10:27

What did you **hear** today from the voice of His word? Psalm 103:20

His Word

Examine It

Apply It

Respond in Prayer

A Good Name Is Better

A good name is better than precious ointment; and the day of death than the day of one's birth.

Ecclesiastes 7:1

Chapter 7:1-14

(1) A good name is better than precious ointment; and the day of death than the day of one's birth.

(2) It is better to go to the house of mourning, than to go to the house of feasting: for that is the end of all men; and the living will lay it to his heart.

(3) Sorrow is better than laughter: for by the sadness of the countenance the heart is made better.

(4) The heart of the wise is in the house of mourning; but the heart of fools is in the house of mirth.

(5) It is better to hear the rebuke of the wise, than for a man to hear the song of fools.

(6) For as the crackling of thorns under a pot, so is the laughter of the fool: this also is vanity.

(7) Surely oppression maketh a wise man mad; and a gift destroyeth the heart.

(8) Better is the end of a thing than the beginning thereof: and the patient in spirit is better than the proud in spirit.

(9) Be not hasty in thy spirit to be angry: for anger resteth in the bosom of fools.

(10) Say not thou, What is the cause that the former days were better than these? for thou dost not enquire wisely concerning this.

(11) Wisdom is good with an inheritance: and by it there is profit to them that see the sun.

(12) For wisdom is a defence, and money is a defence: but the excellency of knowledge is, that wisdom giveth life to them that have it.

(13) Consider the work of God: for who can make that straight, which he hath made crooked?

(14) In the day of prosperity be joyful, but in the day of adversity consider: God also hath set the one over against the other, to the end that man should find nothing after him.

H.E.A.R. *Bible Study Method*

My sheep hear my voice, and I know them, and they follow me: John 10:27

What did you **hear** today from the voice of His word? Psalm 103:20

His Word

Examine It

Apply It

Respond in Prayer

The Contrast of Wisdom and Folly

For there is not a just man upon earth,
that doeth good, and sinneth not.

Ecclesiastes 7:20

Chapter 7:15-29

(15) All things have I seen in the days of my vanity: there is a just man that perisheth in his righteousness, and there is a wicked man that prolongeth his life in his wickedness.

(16) Be not righteous over much; neither make thyself over wise: why shouldest thou destroy thyself?

(17) Be not over much wicked, neither be thou foolish: why shouldest thou die before thy time?

(18) It is good that thou shouldest take hold of this; yea, also from this withdraw not thine hand: for he that feareth God shall come forth of them all.

(19) Wisdom strengtheneth the wise more than ten mighty men which are in the city.

(20) For there is not a just man upon earth, that doeth good, and sinneth not.

(21) Also take no heed unto all words that are spoken; lest thou hear thy servant curse thee:

(22) For oftentimes also thine own heart knoweth that thou thyself likewise hast cursed others.

(23) All this have I proved by wisdom: I said, I will be wise; but it was far from me.

(24) That which is far off, and exceeding deep, who can find it out?

(25) I applied mine heart to know, and to search, and to seek out wisdom, and the reason of things, and to know the wickedness of folly, even of foolishness and madness:

(26) And I find more bitter than death the woman, whose heart is snares and nets, and her hands as bands: whoso pleaseth God shall escape from her; but the sinner shall be taken by her.

(27) Behold, this have I found, saith the preacher, counting one by one, to find out the account:

(28) Which yet my soul seeketh, but I find not: one man among a thousand have I found; but a woman among all those have I not found.

(29) Lo, this only have I found, that God hath made man upright; but they have sought out many inventions.

H.E.A.R. Bible Study Method

My sheep hear my voice, and I know them, and they follow me: John 10:27

What did you **hear** today from the voice of His word? Psalm 103:20

His Word

Examine It

Apply It

Respond in Prayer

Those Who Fear God Will Do Well

Though a sinner do evil an hundred times,
and his day be prolonged, yet surely I know
that it shall be well with them that fear God,
which fear before him:

Ecclesiastes 8:12

Chapter 8

(1) Who is as the wise man? and who knoweth the interpretation of a thing? a man's wisdom maketh his face to shine, and the boldness of his face shall be changed.

(2) I counsel thee to keep the king's commandment, and that in regard of the oath of God.

(3) Be not hasty to go out of his sight: stand not in an evil thing; for he doeth whatsoever pleaseth him.

(4) Where the word of a king is, there is power: and who may say unto him, What doest thou?

(5) Whoso keepeth the commandment shall feel no evil thing: and a wise man's heart discerneth both time and judgment.

(6) Because to every purpose there is time and judgment, therefore the misery of man is great upon him.

(7) For he knoweth not that which shall be: for who can tell him when it shall be?

(8) There is no man that hath power over the spirit to retain the spirit; neither hath he power in the day of death: and there is no discharge in that war; neither shall wickedness deliver those that are given to it.

(9) All this have I seen, and applied my heart unto every work that is done under the sun: there is a time wherein one man ruleth over another to his own hurt.

(10) And so I saw the wicked buried, who had come and gone from the place of the holy, and they were forgotten in the city where they had so done: this is also vanity.

(11) Because sentence against an evil work is not executed speedily, therefore the heart of the sons of men is fully set in them to do evil.

(12) Though a sinner do evil an hundred times, and his days be prolonged, yet surely I know that it shall be well with them that fear God, which fear before him:

(13) But it shall not be well with the wicked, neither shall he prolong his days, which are as a shadow; because he feareth not before God.

(14) There is a vanity which is done upon the earth; that there be just men, unto whom it happeneth according to the work of the wicked; again, there be wicked men, to whom it happeneth according to the work of the righteous: I said that this also is vanity.

(15) Then I commended mirth, because a man hath no better thing under the sun, than to eat, and to drink, and to be merry: for that shall abide with him of his labour the days of his life, which God giveth him under the sun.

(16) When I applied mine heart to know wisdom, and to see the business that is done upon the earth: (for also there is that neither day nor night seeth sleep with his eyes:)

(17) Then I beheld all the work of God, that a man cannot find out the work that is done under the sun: because though a man labour to seek it out, yet he shall not find it; yea further; though a wise man think to know it, yet shall he not be able to find it.

H.E.A.R. *Bible Study Method*

My sheep hear my voice, and I know them, and they follow me: John 10:27

What did you **hear** today from the voice of His word? Psalm 103:20

His Word

Examine It

Apply It

Respond in Prayer

Notes

Notes

Week 3

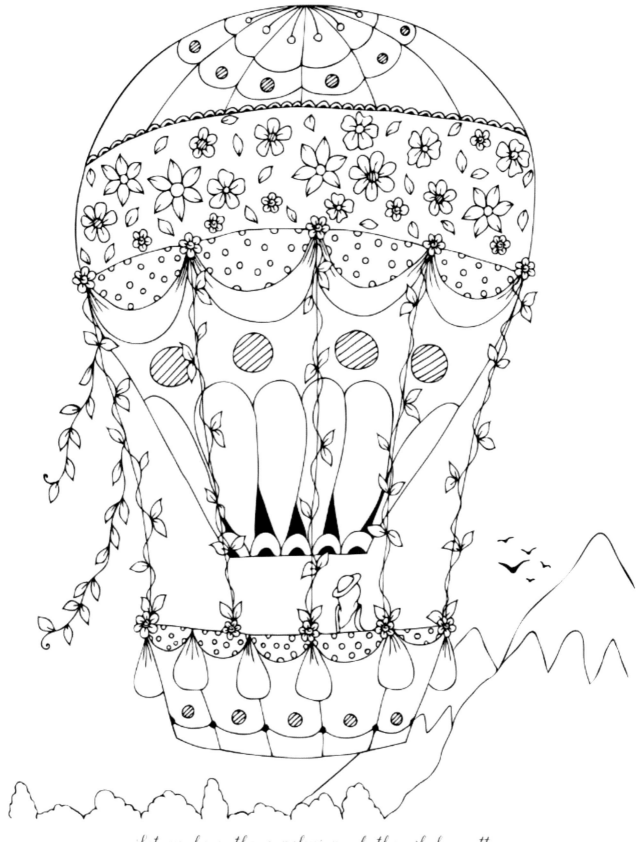

Let us hear the conclusion of the whole matter:
Fear God, and keep his commandments:
for this is the whole duty of man.

Ecclesiastes 12:13

There Is Hope

For to him that is joined to all the living there is hope:

Ecclesiastes 9:4a

Chapter 9

(1) For all this I considered in my heart even to declare all this, that the righteous, and the wise, and their works, are in the hand of God: no man knoweth either love or hatred by all that is before them.

(2) All things come alike to all: there is one event to the righteous, and to the wicked; to the good and to the clean, and to the unclean; to him that sacrificeth, and to him that sacrificeth not: as is the good, so is the sinner; and he that sweareth, as he that feareth an oath.

(3) This is an evil among all things that are done under the sun, that there is one event unto all: yea, also the heart of the sons of men is full of evil, and madness is in their heart while they live, and after that they go to the dead.

(4) For to him that is joined to all the living there is hope: for a living dog is better than a dead lion.

(5) For the living know that they shall die: but the dead know not any thing, neither have they any more a reward; for the memory of them is forgotten.

(6) Also their love, and their hatred, and their envy, is now perished; neither have they any more a portion for ever in any thing that is done under the sun.

(7) Go thy way, eat thy bread with joy, and drink thy wine with a merry heart; for God now accepteth thy works.

(8) Let thy garments be always white; and let thy head lack no ointment.

(9) Live joyfully with the wife whom thou lovest all the days of the life of thy vanity, which he hath given thee under the sun, all the days of thy vanity: for that is thy portion in this life, and in thy labour which thou takest under the sun.

(10) Whatsoever thy hand findeth to do, do it with thy might; for there is no work, nor device, nor knowledge, nor wisdom, in the grave, whither thou goest.

(11) I returned, and saw under the sun, that the race is not to the swift, nor the battle to the strong, neither yet bread to the wise, nor yet riches to men of understanding, nor yet favour to men of skill; but time and chance happeneth to them all.

(12) For man also knoweth not his time: as the fishes that are taken in an evil net, and as the birds that are caught in the snare; so are the sons of men snared in an evil time, when it falleth suddenly upon them.

(13) This wisdom have I seen also under the sun, and it seemed great unto me:

(14) There was a little city, and few men within it; and there came a great king against it, and besieged it, and built great bulwarks against it:

(15) Now there was found in it a poor wise man, and he by his wisdom delivered the city; yet no man remembered that same poor man.

(16) Then said I, Wisdom is better than strength: nevertheless the poor man's wisdom is despised, and his words are not heard.

(17) The words of wise men are heard in quiet more than the cry of him that ruleth among fools.

(18) Wisdom is better than weapons of war: but one sinner destroyeth much good.

H.E.A.R. *Bible Study Method*

My sheep hear my voice, and I know them, and they follow me: John 10:27
What did you **hear** today from the voice of His word? Psalm 103:20

His Word

Examine It

Apply It

Respond in Prayer

Wisdom Is Better Than Folly

The words of a wise man's mouth are gracious;
but the lips of a fool will swallow up himself.

Ecclesiastes 10:12

Chapter 10

(1) Dead flies cause the ointment of the apothecary to send forth a stinking savour: so doth a little folly him that is in reputation for wisdom and honour.

(2) A wise man's heart is at his right hand; but a fool's heart at his left.

(3) Yea also, when he that is a fool walketh by the way, his wisdom faileth him, and he saith to every one that he is a fool.

(4) If the spirit of the ruler rise up against thee, leave not thy place; for yielding pacifieth great offences.

(5) There is an evil which I have seen under the sun, as an error which proceedeth from the ruler:

(6) Folly is set in great dignity, and the rich sit in low place.

(7) I have seen servants upon horses, and princes walking as servants upon the earth.

(8) He that diggeth a pit shall fall into it; and whoso breaketh an hedge, a serpent shall bite him.

(9) Whoso removeth stones shall be hurt therewith; and he that cleaveth wood shall be endangered thereby.

(10) If the iron be blunt, and he do not whet the edge, then must he put to more strength: but wisdom is profitable to direct.

(11) Surely the serpent will bite without enchantment; and a babbler is no better.

(12) The words of a wise man's mouth are gracious; but the lips of a fool will swallow up himself.

(13) The beginning of the words of his mouth is foolishness: and the end of his talk is mischievous madness.

(14) A fool also is full of words: a man cannot tell what shall be; and what shall be after him, who can tell him?

(15) The labour of the foolish wearieth every one of them, because he knoweth not how to go to the city.

(16) Woe to thee, O land, when thy king is a child, and thy princes eat in the morning!

(17) Blessed art thou, O land, when thy king is the son of nobles, and thy princes eat in due season, for strength, and not for drunkenness!

(18) By much slothfulness the building decayeth; and through idleness of the hands the house droppeth through.

(19) A feast is made for laughter, and wine maketh merry: but money answereth all things.

(20) Curse not the king, no not in thy thought; and curse not the rich in thy bedchamber: for a bird of the air shall carry the voice, and that which hath wings shall tell the matter.

H.E.A.R. *Bible Study Method*

My sheep hear my voice, and I know them, and they follow me: John 10:27

What did you **hear** today from the voice of His word? Psalm 103:20

His Word

Examine It

Apply It

Respond in Prayer

Sowing and Reaping

He that observeth the wind shall not sow;
and he that regardeth the clouds shall not reap.

Ecclesiastes 11:4

Chapter 11

(1) Cast thy bread upon the waters: for thou shalt find it after many days.

(2) Give a portion to seven, and also to eight; for thou knowest not what evil shall be upon the earth.

(3) If the clouds be full of rain, they empty themselves upon the earth: and if the tree fall toward the south, or toward the north, in the place where the tree falleth, there it shall be.

(4) He that observeth the wind shall not sow; and he that regardeth the clouds shall not reap.

(5) As thou knowest not what is the way of the spirit, nor how the bones do grow in the womb of her that is with child: even so thou knowest not the works of God who maketh all.

(6) In the morning sow thy seed, and in the evening withhold not thine hand: for thou knowest not whether shall prosper, either this or that, or whether they both shall be alike good.

(7) Truly the light is sweet, and a pleasant thing it is for the eyes to behold the sun:

(8) But if a man live many years, and rejoice in them all; yet let him remember the days of darkness; for they shall be many. All that cometh is vanity.

(9) Rejoice, O young man, in thy youth; and let thy heart cheer thee in the days of thy youth, and walk in the ways of thine heart, and in the sight of thine eyes: but know thou, that for all these things God will bring thee into judgment.

(10) Therefore remove sorrow from thy heart, and put away evil from thy flesh: for childhood and youth are vanity.

H.E.A.R. *Bible Study Method*

My sheep hear my voice, and I know them, and they follow me: John 10:27

What did you **hear** today from the voice of His word? Psalm 103:20

His Word

Examine It

Apply It

Respond in Prayer

The Conclusion

Let us hear the conclusion of the whole matter:
Fear God, and keep his commandments:
for this is the whole duty of man.

Ecclesiastes 12:13

Chapter 12

(1) Remember now thy Creator in the days of thy youth, while the evil days come not, nor the years draw nigh, when thou shalt say, I have no pleasure in them;

(2) While the sun, or the light, or the moon, or the stars, be not darkened, nor the clouds return after the rain:

(3) In the day when the keepers of the house shall tremble, and the strong men shall bow themselves, and the grinders cease because they are few, and those that look out of the windows be darkened,

(4) And the doors shall be shut in the streets, when the sound of the grinding is low, and he shall rise up at the voice of the bird, and all the daughters of musick shall be brought low;

(5) Also when they shall be afraid of that which is high, and fears shall be in the way, and the almond tree shall flourish, and the grasshopper shall be a burden, and desire shall fail: because man goeth to his long home, and the mourners go about the streets:

(6) Or ever the silver cord be loosed, or the golden bowl be broken, or the pitcher be broken at the fountain, or the wheel broken at the cistern.

(7) Then shall the dust return to the earth as it was: and the spirit shall return unto God who gave it.

(8) Vanity of vanities, saith the preacher; all is vanity.

(9) And moreover, because the preacher was wise, he still taught the people knowledge; yea, he gave good heed, and sought out, and set in order many proverbs.

(10) The preacher sought to find out acceptable words: and that which was written was upright, even words of truth.

(11) The words of the wise are as goads, and as nails fastened by the masters of assemblies, which are given from one shepherd.

(12) And further, by these, my son, be admonished: of making many books there is no end; and much study is a weariness of the flesh.

(13) Let us hear the conclusion of the whole matter: Fear God, and keep his commandments: for this is the whole duty of man.

(14) For God shall bring every work into judgment, with every secret thing, whether it be good, or whether it be evil.

H.E.A.R. *Bible Study Method*

My sheep hear my voice, and I know them, and they follow me: John 10:27

What did you **hear** today from the voice of His word? Psalm 103:20

His Word

Examine It

Apply It

Respond in Prayer

Notes

Notes

Made in the USA
Coppell, TX
26 March 2022